RACE CARS

SCIENCE · TECHNOLOGY · ENGINEERING

BY JOSH GREGORY

CHILDREN'S PRESS®

An Imprint of Scholastic Inc.
New York Toronto London Auckland Sydney
Mexico City New Delhi Hong Kong
Danbury, Connecticut

CONTENT CONSULTANT
Scott David Raymond, Technical Director, International Motor Sports Association

PHOTOGRAPHS ©: Alamy Images: 48 (age fotostock Spain, S.L.), 54 left (Amoret Tanner),
45 (Cultura Creative), 4 right, 30 (Dinodia Photos), 18 (DIZ Muenchen GmbH, SueddeutscheZeitung
Photo), 58 (epa european pressphoto agency b.v.), 12, 17 (Everett Collection Historical),
13 (Glasshouse Images), 15, 24 (Heritage Image Partnership Ltd), 11 right (Image Asset Management
Ltd.), 59 (imageBROKER), 34 (Jan Potente), 3, 42 (kolvenbach), 10 right, 11 left (Mary Evans
Picture Library), 8 (Motoring Picture Library), 52 (Richard McDowell), 56 (Steve Nickolas);
AP Images: 44 (Alex Menendez), 22 (Colin E. Braley), 25 top (Len Putnam), 51 (Mel Evans),
43 (Mike McCarn), 49 (Rainier Ehrhardt); Corbis Images/Sutton Images: 28; Ed Shrum: 36, 37;
Getty Images: 26 (Bloomberg), 5 right, 46 (Chris McGrath), 14, 19, 23 (ISC Archives), 53
(Jon Feingersh), cover (Michael Hickey), 6, 20 (NASCAR), 25 bottom (Panoramic Images),
39 (Sports Illustrated), 10 left (SSPL), 50 (Todd Warshaw), 32; Media Bakery/Javier Larrea: 5 left,
38; Shutterstock, Inc.: 29 (Max Earey), 27 (Natursports), 35 (Stanislaw Tokarski),
40 (wavebreakmedia); Superstock, Inc.: 31 (J. W. Alker/imagebroker), 57 (Transtock);
The Image Works: 4 left, 16 (National Motor Museum/HIP), 54 right, 55 left (Professional Sport/
TopFoto), 9 (Roger-Viollet); Thinkstock: 55 right (Inga Nielsen), 41 (Mypurgatoryyears).

LIBRARY OF CONGRESS CATALOGING-IN-PUBLICATION DATA
Gregory, Josh, author.
  Race cars : from concept to consumer / by Josh Gregory.
    pages cm — (Calling all innovators : a career for you?)
  Summary: "Learn about the history of auto racing and find out what it takes to make it in this
exciting career field." — Provided by publisher.
  Audience: Ages 9–12.
  Audience: Grades 4 to 6.
  Includes bibliographical references and index.
  ISBN 978-0-531-20614-0 (lib. bdg.) — ISBN 978-0-531-21073-4 (pbk.)
  1. Automobile racing—Juvenile literature. 2. Automobile racing—History—Juvenile literature.
3. Automobiles, Racing—Juvenile literature. I. Title.
  GV1029.13.G74 2014
  796.72—dc23   2014003565

All rights reserved. Published in 2015 by Children's Press, an imprint of Scholastic Inc.
Printed in the United States of America 113

1 2 3 4 5 6 7 8 9 10 R 24 23 22 21 20 19 18 17 16 15

Science, technology, engineering, arts, and math are the fields that drive innovation. Whether they are finding ways to make our lives easier or developing the latest entertainment, the people who work in these fields are changing the world for the better. Do you have what it takes to join the ranks of today's greatest innovators? Read on to discover if a career in the exciting world of race cars is for you.

Two race cars rush around a corner during a 1933 race through the streets on the Isle of Man.

Rally cars are built to handle a variety of terrain.

Race crews fine tune every single piece of their team's car.

NASCAR teams use trailers to transport cars from the garage to the track.

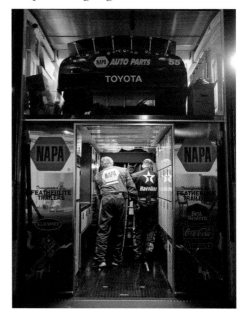

The Daytona 500 is held every February in Daytona Beach, Florida.

CHAPTER ONE

ROAD WARRIORS

Engines roared and tires squealed as a pack of cars came barreling around the corner to start the final lap of the race. For more than three hours, 43 drivers had been competing in the Daytona 500, the biggest annual event of the National Association for Stock Car Racing (NASCAR). The pressure was on as the drivers and their crews battled to win the 200-lap, 500-mile (805 kilometer) race. Engine troubles and crashes had knocked several contenders from the track. Other drivers lagged several laps behind as the top racers came blazing toward the finish line.

The enormous crowd of spectators screamed in excitement as the final seconds of the race played out. All of a sudden, the second-place car pulled out from behind the leader and sped ahead at almost 200 miles per hour (322 kph). Side by side, the two cars were so close that it was hard to tell which was in the lead. The entire crowd was on its feet. It was going to be a finish to remember! But there was a time when most people never imagined cars could be driven at these incredibly fast speeds.

RACES TO REMEMBER

1895	1911	1923	1948
The first automobile race is held in France.	The first Indianapolis 500 is held in Indiana.	The first Le Mans 24-Hour Race is held in France.	The first NASCAR race is held along the beaches in Daytona Beach, Florida.

EARLY INNOVATORS

Cars are an important part of our lives today. It can be difficult to imagine a time before these incredible inventions existed. For hundreds of years before cars were created, people had dreamed of vehicles that were not pulled along by animals. It was not until the late 19th century that this dream became a reality. In 1885, a German engineer named Karl Benz created the first modern automobile. Benz's three-wheeled vehicle was the first to be powered by an **internal combustion engine**. The engine ran on gasoline.

The following year, Benz's fellow Germans Gottlieb Daimler and Wilhelm Maybach created the first gas-powered automobile with four wheels. Within a few years, companies in Europe and the United States were manufacturing cars for sale to the public.

Karl Benz's 1885 three-wheeler was steered by controlling the front wheel.

BERTHA RINGER BENZ

When Karl Benz's automobile failed to sell in the 1880s, Karl's wife, Bertha, packed up their two teenage sons and drove about 65 miles (105 km) without her husband to demonstrate the car's reliability. It was the longest trip yet taken in an automobile. Bertha made emergency repairs along the way and noted ways to improve the car's design. Bertha's trip impressed the public, and the Benz automobile became a success.

LIGHTWEIGHT, WIRE-SPOKE WHEELS

Crowds of spectators lined the streets for the 1895 Paris-Bordeaux race.

RACING IN THE STREET

It didn't take long after cars were invented for people to begin racing them. The first organized automobile competition was held in France in 1894. It was not meant to be a race, but a way to test how reliable the cars would be over a long distance. The competitors began in Paris and traveled about 50 miles (80 km) northwest to the city of Rouen. The first car to arrive had an average speed of just over 10 miles per hour (16 kph). That is slower than a modern-day bicycle race!

The first true automobile race was held on June 13 the following year. It covered a much longer distance, with drivers racing from Paris to the city of Bordeaux and back again. The 732-mile (1,178 km) race took more than two full days to complete. The winner, Émile Levassor, drove a car powered by a Daimler engine.

FIRST THINGS FIRST

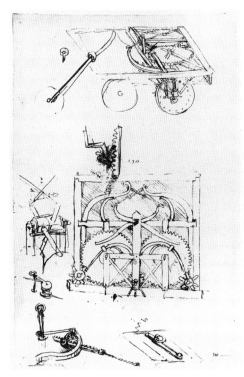

Leonardo da Vinci included sketches of his self-propelled engine design in his notebooks.

UNDER THE HOOD

The idea for automobiles existed hundreds of years before anyone successfully constructed one. The main issue that held back earlier innovators was the lack of an engine powerful and practical enough to propel a vehicle and its passengers. Before the creation of the internal combustion engine, inventors tried to build automobiles using a variety of other power sources.

MAKING PLANS

In the 1400s, famed inventor and artist Leonardo da Vinci sketched out an idea for a car. It was designed to be powered by winding up an elaborate system of springs and gears. While historians believe that this car was never constructed, it is considered to be the first plan for a self-powered vehicle. Around the same time, Italian engineer Roberto Valturio sketched his own plan for a cart that would be powered by windmills. Like da Vinci's vehicle, Valturio's invention was never actually built.

STEAM WAS PRODUCED IN A LARGE BOILER AT THE FRONT OF THE VEHICLE.

EARLY SUCCESSES

It took more than a century for inventors to finally begin having some success with self-powered vehicles. By around 1600, there were wind-powered vehicles in the Netherlands similar to the ones sketched by Robert Valturio. Around 1748, the French inventor Jacques de Vaucanson created a vehicle powered by wind-up clockwork gears.

Camille Jenatzy built his car especially for racing.

STEAM AND ELECTRICITY

In 1769, French inventor Nicolas-Joseph Cugnot built a steam-powered, three-wheeled vehicle. This contraption is often considered to be the first true automobile. Cugnot's creation was large and heavy. It reached a top speed of about 2.5 miles per hour (4 kph). In the following decades, technology improved and was used to build better steam-powered vehicles. Steam-powered tractors and carriages were used in many parts of Europe and the United States.

The 19th century saw the rise of vehicles powered by electricity. The first commercially successful example was created in France in 1881. In 1899, an electric car built by Belgian inventor and racer Camille Jenatzy became the first automobile to reach 68 miles per hour (109 kph). Electric cars had some popularity during the 19th century and early 20th century. However, the lack of places to charge batteries eventually made them less successful than gas-powered cars. ✸

Like other early self-powered vehicles, Nicolas-Joseph Cugnot's vehicle had three wheels.

Charles Duryea sits in one of his and his brother's inventions.

AMERICA HITS THE ROAD

Europe was not the only place where people went car crazy in the late 1800s. Americans wanted to hit the road, too. Many inventors worked to create their own automobiles. The first to achieve real success were brothers Charles and Frank Duryea. The Duryeas completed a design for a gas-powered car in 1891. They successfully drove their creation through the streets of Springfield, Massachusetts, in 1893.

The United States saw its first automobile race on Thanksgiving Day 1895. Racers sped through Illinois along Lake Michigan from Chicago to the nearby town of Evanston and back for a total of about 54 miles (87 km). Six drivers competed in the race, but only two made it all the way back to the finish line. The winning car was built by the Duryeas and driven by Frank.

MOTORS FOR THE MASSES

Until the early 20th century, cars were not common items. Only wealthy people could afford them, and it took a long time for factories to build them. That all changed with the work of American inventor and businessman Henry Ford. Ford decided to build a car that the average person could afford.

Ford's car, the Model T, was first sold in 1908. It was built using Ford's remarkably efficient **mass production** process. Over the next two decades, Ford sold nearly 15 million of the cars, most of them in the United States. Almost overnight, the country saw major changes thanks to Ford's innovation. Roads and highways began to crisscross the nation. Cities and towns spread as it became easier to get from one place to another. With so many people behind the wheel, racing became more popular than ever.

The Model T made cars accessible to more people than ever before.

Henry Ford races against Alexander Winton at Grosse Pointe, Michigan.

FORD AT THE FINISH LINE

Before striking it big as the most successful automobile manufacturer in the world, Henry Ford saw success inventing high-powered experimental race cars. He was personally uninterested in racing for the most part. However, he knew that fast cars would attract attention from the public, who at the time mostly thought of automobiles as toys.

SWEEPSTAKES

In early 1901, Ford constructed a technologically advanced race car that he named Sweepstakes. During a test run in July of that year, Ford was able to reach a speed of 72 miles per hour (116 kph). Confident in his car's speed, he challenged fellow automaker Alexander Winton to a race. On October 10, Ford and Winton met at the starting line of a dirt track in Grosse Pointe, Michigan. The spectators expected Ford to lose. Winton was known for his racing skills, while Ford had never raced before. Despite being the underdog, Ford won the 10-mile (16 km) race with an average speed of almost 45 miles per hour (72 kph). His plan of attracting attention through racing was a major success. As news of the race spread, investors began offering him money to fund the Ford Motor Company.

The Ford car that Barney Oldfield (left) drove was originally named Arrow before being changed to 999.

THE FORD 999

The next year, Ford built a pair of twin race cars, both named the 999. This new model was an engineering marvel, able to reach speeds far beyond anything that had been built previously. On October 25, 1902, racer Barney Oldfield set a record in the 999 when he became the first person to complete one lap around a 1-mile-long (1.6 km) track in less than a minute.

Ford himself set another speed record while driving that car's twin in January 1904. While zooming across a frozen lake, he moved at more than 91 miles per hour (146 kph). No car had ever reached such a tremendous speed! ☀

NEW COMPANIES

With the success of Ford, Benz, and Daimler, many other companies were formed to meet the growing demand for cars. In France, Peugeot and Renault were two of the first manufacturers to find success. Fiat, Maserati, and Alfa Romeo were among the early automotive giants in Italy. All of these manufacturers built cars used in 20th-century racing, and they continue to produce automobiles today.

In the wake of Ford's success, the United States became a hotbed of automobile manufacturing. Specifically, the city of Detroit, Michigan, became known as the Motor City for its domination of the industry. Ford made the city his headquarters. So did William C. Durant, the founder of General Motors. General Motors grew rapidly after its creation in 1908. It eventually owned such legendary American car companies as Chevrolet, Oldsmobile, Buick, and Cadillac.

Two drivers, both in Alfa Romeos, race toward the finish line in 1933 on the Isle of Man.

Driver W. K. Vanderbilt Jr. drives his Mercedes during a 1908 race.

A FORK IN THE ROAD

In the early days of racing, cars weren't usually built specifically for the track. Instead, most race cars were **prototypes** for future production models. Car manufacturers saw racing as a great way to test out cars they would later be selling to the public.

This all changed as racing grew popular as a sport and more people began using cars for everyday travel. Racers simply wanted their cars to go as fast as possible and handle well. They wanted to take advantage of the latest technology to get more speed. Average people wanted vehicles that were safe, reliable, and comfortable. As a result, car manufacturers began designing and building race cars separately from standard models in the late 1910s and early 1920s.

The Grand Prix in Monaco has built a reputation as one of the most difficult and famous Grands Prix since the first race there in 1929.

GRANDS PRIX

In Europe, the most popular form of racing during the early 20th century was the Grand Prix (French for "grand prize"). Grand Prix races were usually held on long routes of closed roads instead of tracks. The first one was held in France in 1906. Racers completed 12 laps around a 64-mile (103 km) **circuit** over the course of two days. Soon, countries throughout Europe were hosting a variety of Grand Prix events every year.

In the early 1920s, the rules for Grand Prix races were limited to include only **open-wheeled**, single-seat cars. These rules were enforced by an organization that came to be known as the Fédération Internationale de l'Automobile (FIA). The FIA has overseen racing events around the world since its founding in 1904.

RACING IN THE UNITED STATES

In 1911, the first Indianapolis 500 race was held at the Indianapolis Motor Speedway in Indiana. Unlike most of the European Grand Prix events, the Indy 500 was held on a track. The race was a huge success. It has been held almost every year since, aside from short breaks during World War I (1914–1918) and World War II (1939–1945).

As the years went on, auto racing became more professional, and several major organizations formed to govern the sport. Grand Prix races on closed-off roads remained popular in Europe as Americans flocked to races held on tracks. Open-wheeled cars came to dominate European racing, while Americans tended to prefer stock cars, or modified versions of the cars produced for everyday consumers.

Racers complete an opening pace lap at the 1955 Indy 500.

Fans greet driver Jimmie Johnson before a race at the Daytona International Speedway.

CHAPTER TWO

TODAY'S RACERS

These days, auto racing is no longer the hot new thing. However, its age has done nothing to diminish the excitement it inspires in its fans. For decades, automobile racing has been one of the world's most popular sports. It has a rich history filled with long-standing traditions. Millions of race fans attend races, watch events on television, and proudly wear merchandise bearing the logos and numbers of their favorite drivers. These fans pour billions of dollars into the racing industry every year. They tune in to see the fastest cars and the best drivers compete in high-stakes races around the world. Today's drivers zoom around many different tracks and courses in countless types of automobiles. There are varieties of racing to meet every fan's taste, whether it's on a straight and simple track or one full of twists and turns, lasting a few brief seconds or several days, or won through unbelievable **acceleration** or careful strategies and impressive endurance.

TOP TRACKS

1907	1909	1929	1959
Brooklands, in Surrey, England, becomes the first track built especially for auto racing.	The Indianapolis Motor Speedway opens.	The streets of Monaco, France, are used to host a Grand Prix for the first time.	The Daytona International Speedway hosts its first race.

Today, there are dozens of NASCAR tracks across the United States.

SPEEDY STOCK CARS

Stock car racing has been the United States' most popular form of racing for several decades. Today, the sport is dominated by the National Association for Stock Car Auto Racing, better known as NASCAR. NASCAR oversees several racing **series**. Its biggest is the NASCAR Sprint Cup Series. Races in this series are held almost every weekend between February and November. Drivers earn points for their performance in each race, and the driver with the most points at the end of the season is the champion.

Most NASCAR tracks are roughly oval shaped. Others are full of twists and turns. The cars used in NASCAR races are extremely fast, reaching speeds of more than 200 miles per hour (322 kph). They are very heavy, and they lack the sleek shapes of many other types of race cars. Despite their size, however, they still have very responsive **handling**. Some of today's most famous NASCAR drivers include Jimmie Johnson, Matt Kenseth, and Dale Earnhardt Jr.

FROM DIRT ROADS TO STADIUMS

Racer and businessman William "Big Bill" France formed NASCAR in 1948. Stock car racing had been popular for many years before that. However, it was very disorganized. There were no consistent rules from race to race. Races simply occurred as expert drivers challenged each other to prove their skills on dirt tracks. NASCAR changed all of that, overseeing events and regulating the tracks and cars that could be used. The organization also kept track of race results and awarded prizes to champions. By the end of the 1970s, NASCAR races were seen on television and sponsored by major companies.

At first, NASCAR cars were true stock cars. They were the same cars that rolled off the assembly lines and made their way to the dealerships, where anyone could purchase them. However, NASCAR soon began allowing race teams to modify their cars to make them safer and faster. Today's NASCAR stock cars have very little in common with production models. They are built from scratch by race teams.

Driver Red Byron (left) talks with Big Bill France before a race.

FROM THIS TO THAT

Driver Alessandro Cagno races along a road in Dieppe, France, in 1908.

ROADS AND TRACKS

Race fans pay a lot of attention to cars. They debate the benefits and drawbacks of different car parts. They marvel at the speed and handling of a well-built automobile. However, cars aren't the only impressive technology involved in automobile racing. The roads and tracks on which drivers compete are just as important to the results of a race as the cars are.

GETTING STARTED

The earliest automobile races were held wherever drivers could find room. This usually meant that cars would race along the same, regular roads that horse-drawn carts and carriages used at the time. Some of these races were even held on roads that were open to other traffic. Regular traffic would ride right alongside the racers.

Other early races were held on tracks. However, there were no tracks designed specifically for the speed and maneuverability of cars at first. Instead, drivers competed on tracks that had originally been built for horse races.

Brooklands was not the first track used for race cars, but it was the first track specifically built for automobile racing.

PURPOSE-BUILT

The first track built specifically for racing was opened in 1907 in Surrey, England. The circuit, named Brooklands, was 2.75 miles (4.4 km) long. It was engineered to allow cars to build up as much speed as possible, with two long **straightaways** and two banked, or sloped, sections. Crowds gathered at the track to watch cars race along the concrete circuit, reaching speeds that were very impressive for the time. Brooklands held auto races until World War I broke out in 1914.

The Indianapolis Motor Speedway oval track is 2.5 miles (4 km) around.

INDIANAPOLIS MOTOR SPEEDWAY

The Indianapolis Motor Speedway opened in 1909. It remains one of the world's most famous racetracks. The speedway has an oval shape that is almost rectangular. Unlike many tracks, it does not have especially steep banks on its turns. That doesn't make it any less exciting, however. The track is home to such events as the Indianapolis 500 and NASCAR's Brickyard 400, among others. It has seating for more than 250,000 spectators, making it the world's largest sports venue.

DAYTONA INTERNATIONAL SPEEDWAY

The Daytona International Speedway is another of the world's most famous tracks. It has an almost triangular oval shape. Each of its four turns is banked at a steep 31-degree angle. This allows drivers to jet out of corners and into straightaways at tremendous speeds, making for very exciting races. The track is home to the Daytona 500, NASCAR's biggest annual race. ✳

OUT IN THE OPEN

While stock cars dominate much of the racing industry in America, they are far from the only kind of race cars. Many styles of racing rely on open-wheeled cars. Instead of having wheels that lie underneath **fenders** as stock cars do, the wheels of an open-wheeled car stick out from the sides of the body. As a result, the cars sit very low to the ground. They also tend to have very **aerodynamic** shapes. These features help make the cars very fast and **maneuverable**.

Open-wheeled cars are sometimes also known as single-seater cars. This is because they only have enough room inside for one person: the driver. In addition, the driver of an open-wheeled car does not usually sit completely inside of a car the way a stock car driver does. Instead, the top of the **cockpit** is exposed to open air. The top of a driver's helmet can be seen sticking out from the car.

THE DRIVER'S HEAD STICKS OUT OF THE COCKPIT IN AN F1 CAR.

Drivers in open-cockpit race cars are generally required to wear helmets that fully cover their head and face.

F1 drivers race around a corner at a Grand Prix race in Spain.

THE WINNING FORMULA

The highest level of open-wheeled racing today is Formula One, or F1. Overseen by the FIA, Formula One racing grew out of the traditional European Grand Prix racing of the early 20th century. During an F1 season, racers compete in a series of Grands Prix. Some Grands Prix are held on closed roads, or roads that are blocked off from normal traffic. Other Grands Prix take place on tracks that are designed to resemble roads. F1 cars and drivers receive points for race performance, similar to NASCAR. However, in F1, separate championships are awarded to drivers and constructor teams.

Constructor teams are the people who build F1 cars. They take advantage of the newest technology to make their cars as fast, safe, and maneuverable as possible. **Engineers** carefully design car shapes to be as aerodynamic as fighter jets. Like jets, F1 cars even have wings. However, jet wings create positive lift, which causes the aircraft to leave the ground. F1 cars are designed to create negative lift, which presses the car to the road as the vehicle races along at remarkable speeds.

MODERN MARVEL

Alan van der Merwe became the world's fastest F1 driver on a track in 2006.

THE NEED FOR SPEED

From the very beginning, automobile racing grew out of the desire to drive as fast as possible. The challenge of designing and building the fastest cars has pushed the sport forward throughout its long and storied history. Today, automakers are always working to make their cars faster than ever before.

THE FASTEST ON THE TRACK

In 2006, racer Alan van der Merwe set a world record by pushing his Honda F1 car to an average speed of about 221 miles per hour (356 kph) during a test run. The Honda team worked tirelessly to fine-tune every detail of the car, such as increasing the tires' **traction** for better handling, to reach this incredible speed. No other F1 car has been able to officially match it so far.

THE FASTEST ON THE STREET

Some of the fastest cars in the world today aren't technically race cars. They are production models that people can purchase, provided they can afford such expensive vehicles. Guinness World Records awarded the record for the world's fastest production car to the Bugatti Veyron Super Sport. In a speed test in July 2010, the car reached a top speed of 267 miles per hour (430 kph)! However, the record was withdrawn in 2013. It was revealed that the production version of the car had technology that limited its top speed to 258 miles per hour (415 kph). This is done to keep the car's tires from exploding at high speeds!

In 2013, a car called the Hennessey Venom GT reached a top speed of 265.7 miles per hour (427.6 kph). Even though it doesn't quite reach the Veyron Super Sport's speeds, it is technically the fastest car money can buy. It can accelerate from 0 to 186 miles per hour (299 kph) in less than 14 seconds! ☀

The Bugatti Veyron Super Sport sells for roughly $2.5 million dollars.

RALLY RACING

One of the most unique forms of racing is rallying. Rally racers drive modified versions of street cars across an incredible variety of environments and road conditions. The goal of a rally is to complete a number of closed-road courses called special stages as quickly as possible. Drivers can go as fast as they want to inside the special stages. However, racers use public roads to travel between each special stage. There, they drive alongside regular vehicles and obey traffic laws.

Rally cars do not go as fast as most other race cars. Their maximum speed in the special stages is usually below 140 miles per hour (225 kph). However, this lower speed does not make rallying any less exciting. Special stages are often held on a variety of different off-road surfaces, from rocky dirt trails to icy paths!

DANIEL ELENA

Sébastien Loeb is the world's most successful rally driver, with 78 rally wins and nine back-to-back world titles. He accomplished this with the help of his codriver, Daniel Elena. The two paired up in 1998 and started winning races in 2002. As codriver, Elena supplied Loeb with detailed descriptions of a stage's route and conditions. Loeb used this information to know when and how much to break, accelerate, or turn.

Controlling a car on the difficult terrain of a rally course requires a lot of skill.

Drag racers must react quickly when the light turns green so they can start moving at the earliest possible moment.

SHORT AND SPEEDY

Another popular form of racing today is drag racing. Drag racing is very different from most other types of racing. Instead of driving along a track with twists and turns, trying to pass the cars ahead of them, drivers face off on two short, straight, parallel tracks. This means that a drag race is based almost entirely on a car's ability to accelerate very quickly. When the light turns green at the starting line, the two cars launch forward all at once. The drivers do not steer. They simply try to reach top speeds as fast as possible. Even though a drag race only lasts a few seconds, cars can reach speeds of more than 300 miles per hour (483 kph)! After they cross the finish line, drivers release parachutes from the back of their cars to help slow the cars down.

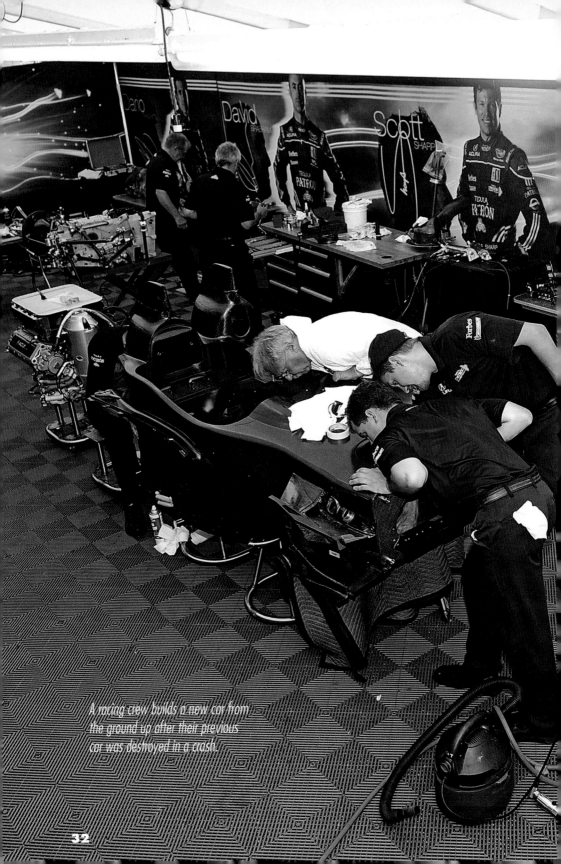

A racing crew builds a new car from the ground up after their previous car was destroyed in a crash.

CHAPTER THREE

MEET THE CREW

Racing fans all know the names of their favorite racers, but these daring drivers aren't the only people on a racing team. It takes an entire team of skilled, dedicated workers to build and maintain a modern race car. Each team member has his or her own role to play in maximizing the speed, efficiency, and safety of the team car. Without this crew of specialists, a driver would be going nowhere.

Most professional race cars are built from scratch in the team's shop. From a car's initial design to its construction and its upkeep, a crew faces a variety of challenges. Race cars are highly complicated machines, and even the tiniest details can affect the results of a race. Race car builders work hard both mentally and physically to keep drivers safe and help them blow away the competition on the track. All of these workers rely on a detailed understanding of cars and racing, as well as on their math and science knowledge.

FORMULA ONE FIRSTS

1946	1950	1953	1976
The first F1 race is held.	Great Britain hosts the first F1 world championship race.	Argentina hosts the first F1 Grand Prix to be held outside of Europe.	Japan hosts Asia's first F1 Grand Prix.

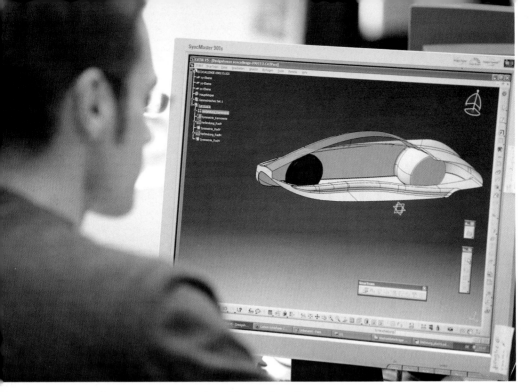

CAD software is a common tool in all kinds of car design.

MECHANICAL ENGINEERS

Racing teams rely on mechanical engineers when it comes to designing cars, parts, and tools. These engineers have detailed knowledge of machinery, math, and physics. They plan out every detail of a car's components, or parts, from its engine to its **suspension**, down to the smallest part. They experiment with different materials to make a car lighter or safer. They also work to make cars as aerodynamic as possible so the vehicles can cut through the air to reach amazing speeds.

Engineers use computer-aided design (CAD) software to help them draw plans for new parts and figure out how the parts will go together. Computer simulations use math to predict how the designs will perform on the track. Once the engineers have a plan put together, they create charts, diagrams, and manuals to help the rest of the team build and maintain the car.

SHOP MECHANICS

The job of a race car mechanic is very similar to that of a mechanic who works on everyday cars. However, race car mechanics are the best of the best. Race teams rely on them to find problems with a car, come up with solutions, and perform repairs quickly. Pro race teams might include several mechanics, each with a different specialty. For example, one mechanic might work only on engines, while another might focus on the car's steering or brakes. This sort of specialization allows each mechanic to become a high-level expert in that field. Such experience allows the mechanic to work faster and come up with solutions that others might not consider.

Mechanics are constantly fixing any problems and fine-tuning a race car to keep it in top shape.

Ed Shrum is a race car mechanic and driver. He races at events throughout the country in a car that he and his team built from the ground up.

When did you start thinking you wanted to work on race cars? Did any person or event inspire that career choice? I started working on cars as a hobby while stationed with the U.S. Navy. The navy mechanics were a close group, and we often went to races together. We met legendary drag racer John Force and his crew in Pomona, California, and the feeling of building cars specifically for racing started to grow.

Ed Shrum (center) stands with members of his race team, Crew Chief John Miles (left) and additional driver Dan Stalzer.

What kinds of classes should a would-be race car mechanic look to take in middle school, high school, and beyond? Students should take math courses such as **trigonometry**, algebra, and geometry. Engineering would be nice, too. Metal shop and auto shop classes give you some basic design and repair training.

What other projects and jobs did you do in school and your work life before the opportunity to work on race cars came along? How did that work prepare you? In high school, I had my goals set for a totally different job. Not having the money for college changed my path in life. [Since being] in the racing field, I have embraced the chance to develop the skills that are needed to fix the complex new cars and the race cars of today.

As a senior master technician for Ford, I get to see new technology implemented frequently, and continuing education plays a part in keeping my mind focused. The more you learn, the better prepared you are for unexpected challenges.

Do you have a particular project that you're especially proud of or that you think really took your work to another level? Last year, my team and I embarked on a challenge to build a car from scratch. We built it from the ground up, including the **chassis**, engine, and drivetrain [the parts that deliver power from the engine to the wheels]. Then we took it to the track to see if we could be competitive. It started out as a 1972 Toyota Corolla and has evolved into an SCCA [Sports Car Club of America] road racing Grand Touring Lite racer.

It takes teamwork to keep a race car in competitive shape for the track. Does working as part of a team come naturally to you, or was it something you had to work on? Being a team player has come from my experience as a driver as well as a crew member. It is always a work in progress to keep everyone on the same page.

Teamwork is very important to keeping these cars at their peak. The driver has to be able to communicate to the team what he feels while driving. Then we as his crew have to come up with a course of action to make it better. If we couldn't work together, the car would not be very competitive.

If you had unlimited resources to build whatever kind of car you wanted to, what would you do? I would love to build a car for the 24 Hours of Daytona race. This race really tells the story of reliability and endurance. It must be a real joy to make it to the end. Just making it into the field is an engineering feat of its own, but to last the whole 24-hour race with multiple drivers and crew members working nonstop has to be overwhelming.

What advice would you give a young person who wants to work on race cars one day? Start early. Go to the track and talk to the people working in the pits. Find the thing that drives your passion. Get involved and test the waters. There are all kinds of racing, and there is always a need for a warm body to help. Not all racing leads to a lucrative [profitable] lifestyle. Sometimes it is just the thrill of the race that drives people. ☀

FABRICATORS AND BODY HANGERS

Because race cars are often highly customized, they cannot be built using the same pieces you might find at an auto parts store. Instead, experts called fabricators usually build race car parts from scratch. Fabricators cut and shape pieces of metal, carbon fiber, and other materials to meet the specifications outlined by the team's engineers. As the team puts a car together, fabricators can make small adjustments in a hurry to meet the car's needs.

The outer layer of a race car is called its shell. This is the smooth, colored exterior that shows the racer's number and sponsor logos. Underneath the shell are a frame and all of the parts that make the car work. Shells are attached to the frame by specialized workers called body hangers. They must attach the shell securely to very specific points on the frame to make sure the car is safe and functional.

Mechanics work on the body of a car in Formula 3000, which is a stepping stone toward F1 racing.

A large racing team means there are a lot of people in the garage at one time. A foreperson keeps tasks and people organized.

THE FOREPERSON

With so many people working together in a race car shop, a strong leader is needed to keep the process organized. This duty falls to a team member called the shop foreperson. The foreperson plans all of the work to be done by the rest of the team. He or she keeps track of what needs to be done and in which order. Race car teams often have just a few days between races, and a lot needs to be done during this time. The foreperson makes sure everything stays on schedule.

The foreperson also works to communicate information between the workers and the other members of the race team. For example, a driver who has a problem with the car during a race might discuss the issue with the foreperson, who then explains the issue to the workers in the shop.

THE ARTISTIC SIDE

Special tablets make it easier for graphic designers to draw or adjust their work on the computer.

COLORFUL CREATIONS

When you're watching a race, cars zoom by so quickly that it can be hard to focus on what the vehicles actually look like. However, it you take a peek at a race car when it is parked, you will notice a beautiful display of colors, logos, and other eye-catching designs. These colorful coverings are designed and applied by some of the most artistic members of a race team.

DARING DESIGNS

The designs on a race car's shell are carefully planned out by creative workers called graphic designers. Graphic designers work in a wide variety of fields, from Web design to advertising. They are experts in choosing just the right shapes, colors, and fonts to give a certain message. For example, one race team might want its car to look tough and aggressive. Another might want its car to look futuristic. Graphic designers also know which colors go well together. This helps them keep cars from looking like a mess of random graphics.

PUTTING DOWN PAINT

Once a design has been created, a car's shell is carefully painted piece by piece. The process of painting a race car can take as long as two days. Painters start by making sure the shell is extremely clean. Then they apply a layer of paint primer. This is a substance that helps the paint stick to the car evenly. Cars are then painted layer by layer. This process is usually done by automatic machines that have the car's design programmed into them. Because paint adds weight to the car, the amount of paint used is carefully controlled. Once the painting is finished, the car's body is covered in a protective layer. This keeps the car shiny and smooth, and keeps the paint from flaking off.

Today, car designs are sometimes applied using something called a wrap. Instead of painting, a race team covers the car in a thin layer of colored vinyl. This process takes only a few hours, which is much faster than painting. Wraps can also be more lightweight than paint. ✳

Painters wear special masks to protect themselves from harmful fumes.

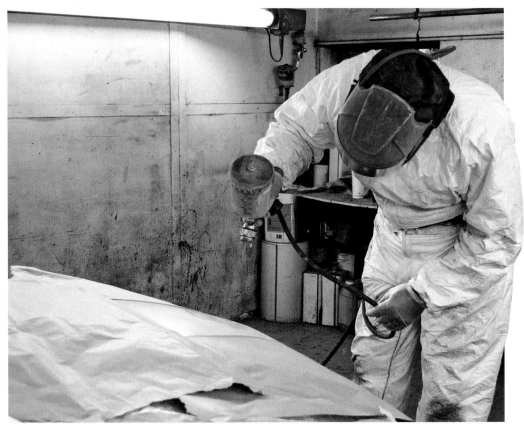

FUEL

JACK TO LIFT CAR

Several members of the pit crew all work at once during a pit stop.

IN THE PIT

Even after a car is ready for race day, an entire crew of talented
workers is on hand to keep it in top shape. This group is the pit
crew. For most types of racing, the pit crew is made up of the same
mechanics who maintain the cars. In NASCAR, pit crew members
are separate from the maintenance team.

Before a race starts, pit crews perform final tests and make sure
cars are safe and ready to go. During many kinds of races, drivers
must pull off the track partway through to keep their cars in fighting
shape. These detours are called pit stops. Each one takes up valuable
time. A pit crew must make the stop go as quickly as possible. As
soon as a driver pulls into the pit, each crew member is off and
running to complete his or her assigned task. One person refuels
while another cleans the windshield. One person lifts the car with a
jack as others remove the used tires and put on fresh ones. A skilled
NASCAR pit crew can complete a pit stop in less than 15 seconds.
Stops at the Indy 500 might take less than five seconds, and F1 crews
can get drivers back on the track in less than two seconds!

THE COACH AND THE CHIEF

The pit crew functions like any well-trained sports team. Each player knows his or her position. The members also practice their timing and teamwork constantly, even on days when there are no races. Like any good team, they have a coach who helps plan strategies and figures out who works best in which position.

The crew chief is another important leader on a race team. He or she oversees all preparations for a race and manages the team's employees both in the garage and in the pit. Exact duties often vary from team to team. Some crew chiefs might determine what kind of tires a car needs to run on a certain track or how the car's suspension should be tuned for a given race. When other team members have questions, they come to the chief for answers.

COMMUNICATIONS
HEADSET

NASCAR driver Jimmie Johnson (right) talks with his crew chief during practice before a race.

DARING DRIVERS

Last but not least, there is the team member who spends the most time in the spotlight. A race car driver has a unique and extremely difficult job. Handling a high-powered automobile at top speeds requires superhuman reflexes and a lot of quick thinking. Racers must strategize the best times to try and pass opponents while also preventing other racers from passing them.

Drivers must keep themselves in good physical shape. Driving at high speeds for hours at a time puts a lot of stress on a driver's body. A driver's heart beats very fast during a race, just like a cyclist, a runner, or any other athlete. Even under this intense physical stress, racers must be able to stay fully alert and strong throughout an entire race. If they weren't able to concentrate and perform at a high level, they would put themselves at risk of crashing into a wall or another car.

Racers such as NASCAR driver Danica Patrick are required to wear special safety gear, including fire-resistant suits.

Hands-on experience is a great way to learn how cars work.

LEARNING THE RIGHT SKILLS

If you're interested in working for a race team one day, you will need a lot of education and training. Start early by spending as much time around cars as you can. If your parents or neighbors work on their cars at home, ask if you can watch or even help. As you grow older, you can take shop and auto repair classes to learn more about how to keep a car in running condition.

You should also take as many math and science courses as you can. These subjects will help you learn why cars work the way they do and how their design affects their performance. Math and science are especially important if you hope to become a mechanical engineer. Engineers need college degrees before they can work for a pro race team. Other team members usually need either a college degree or certification from a technical school.

NASCAR team members load equipment onto a truck before heading to a race location.

CHAPTER FOUR

FROM THE GARAGE TO THE TRACK

B uilding and maintaining a modern race car takes an incredible amount of work. All of a car's individual components must work together as a single machine. Race teams replace car parts, take huge sections apart, and rebuild their vehicles constantly to stay competitive. For example, NASCAR teams tear down and rebuild their cars almost entirely in between each weekend race. This allows them to correct any issues they had in previous races. It also gives them the opportunity to customize the car to perform on the exact conditions of the track where the next race will be held. In addition, race teams often travel with multiple cars, in case a backup is needed. This means they are often working on several cars at the same time!

TECHNOLOGICAL FEATS

1895	1933	1968	2014
Édouard Michelin is the first racer to use air-filled tires.	Chet "Radio" Gardner is the first driver to successfully use a radio to communicate with his crew during a race.	Wings are added to F1 cars for the first time.	The FIA hosts the first electric Grand Prix, the Formula E Championship.

CHOOSING A CHASSIS

Building a race car all starts with the chassis. The chassis is the metal frame that lies beneath the car's body. It is like the car's skeleton. It provides the basic structure of a race car, and all other parts are built onto it. The chassis needs to be very strong to hold the car together and keep the driver safe in the event of an accident. It is made of

many steel tubes that are **welded** together. Welding forms a strong bond between the pieces of metal so they will not come apart during a race.

In a car with an enclosed cockpit, some metal tubes form a part of the chassis called the roll cage. This is an important safety feature. The roll cage is a tough frame around the cockpit. It keeps the roof or sides of the car from caving in if the car is flipped over in a crash.

Formula 3000 mechanics work on their car's chassis.

All parts of a race car's body need to be attached securely.

BUILDING A BODY

Once the chassis is built, the team's fabricators and body hangers build the body around it. The pieces of a race car's body are made from flat sheets of metal. Fabricators use **templates** to trace outlines of each body piece onto the metal sheets. They then use special tools to cut out the shapes. Because race cars do not have many flat surfaces, the body pieces must be bent into precise shapes after they are cut out. The pieces must fit the exact curves of the chassis so they can be bolted on tightly. Fabricators rely on giant rolling machines to help them with the curving process. Once the pieces are ready, body hangers bolt them to the chassis. Then the workers weld all of the seams together so there are no cracks between the different pieces. This helps make the car more aerodynamic.

WHERE THE MAGIC HAPPENS

NASCAR TECHNICAL INSTITUTE

In addition to having experience behind the wheel and in the garage, most race team members attend technical schools to sharpen their skills. Many schools offer programs where students can learn how to build and maintain cars. For example, NASCAR partnered with the Universal Technical Institute (UTI) in 2002 to create a program designed specially for training future NASCAR team members. Located in Mooresville, North Carolina, the NASCAR Technical Institute has set many students on the road to a career in auto racing.

Becoming part of a skillful pit crew requires a lot of training and practice.

A DEMANDING CHALLENGE

The NASCAR Technical Institute program is a 15-week course of study that students can take in addition to UTI's standard automotive technology training program. This means that they learn all of the basic skills needed to work on everyday cars. At the same time, they can study the special skills needed to build and maintain professional-level stock cars, too. Students learn how to design and fabricate stock car bodies and work with high-powered, custom-built engines. They also go through pit crew training, where they learn about NASCAR's rules and a pit crew's many responsibilities.

It takes hard work to even earn a place on a NASCAR team, much less help bring that team to victory.

THE STARTING LINE OF A CAREER

Graduates of the NASCAR Technical Institute are not guaranteed to land top positions on pro race teams as soon as they graduate. Many of them begin their careers working on regular cars while establishing a career in racing. Others start out in low-level positions on race teams or for NASCAR itself. It is not easy to become a professional race team member, but with enough hard work and a little bit of raw talent, skilled workers can make their way up to the big leagues. Some of the program's graduates work on the teams of NASCAR's top drivers! ☀

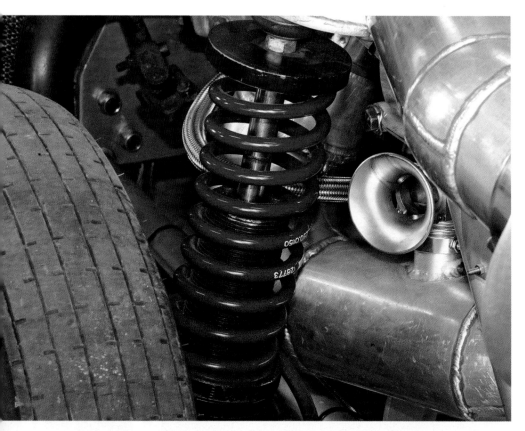

This spring and the shock absorber it surrounds are part of a drag racer's suspension system.

A SMOOTH RIDE

With the main body of the car in place, the team adds the various systems that turn the vehicle from a hunk of metal into a lightning-fast racer. One of the first systems to be installed in a car is the suspension. The suspension is a collection of springs and shock absorbers that connect the chassis to the car's wheels and axles. The suspension plays a major role in the car's handling abilities. It also keeps the car's tires in contact with the road while the rest of the car bounces around as it barrels through corners or runs across bumps. Each individual part of the suspension can be adjusted to meet the needs of a certain track or fit a driver's personal preferences.

IN CONTROL

A car's handling is also greatly affected by its steering and brake systems. Race car builders connect the car's steering wheel to the complex steering system on its front wheels. They also install the car's brakes. Different brake requirements are needed for different types of races. When a track has many twists and turns, drivers must brake more often to maneuver around the corners. Oval-shaped tracks with wide curves and long straightaways barely require any braking at all. When racers do hit the brakes, they generate a great deal of heat as the car's brake **rotors** rub against the brake pads. Race car brakes sometimes get so hot that they glow orange and red! Race teams install special cooling systems to keep the brakes from overheating during a race.

Race teams can adjust a car's steering to suit a track and a driver's personal preferences.

LASTING CONTRIBUTIONS

John Dunlop created a successful company that produced bicycle tires.

BURNING RUBBER

Tires are one of the most crucial features of any vehicle, from your bicycle or family car to the world's fastest racers. Without intact, well-inflated tires, none of these vehicles would be able to travel very far. Tires affect a race car's traction, which in turn affects the car's handling. While tires come in many shapes and sizes, they all rely on the same basic principles. Tires are made mostly of rubber. They wrap around a vehicle's wheels and are filled with air. This allows the vehicle to better grip the surface it is driving on. It also absorbs some shock.

TIRES THROUGH TIME

The earliest known tires were designed in 1845 by Scottish inventor Robert William Thomson. They were made of leather and wrapped around the wheels of a horse-drawn carriage. However, tires did not become popular until later in the century. In 1887, Scots inventor John Dunlop created rubber tires for his son's tricycle. Dunlop's tires quickly became popular among bicycle manufacturers, as they made cycling a much smoother experience than it had been. Car inventors of the late 19th

century soon saw the potential for tires on their own designs. Since then, tires have been an important part of all automobiles.

TYPES OF TIRES

Today, there are many different types of tires. They are designed to fit a wide variety of vehicles and to operate under varied conditions. For example, a tire's **treads** affect the way it handles on different surfaces. Off-road vehicles have big treads that allow them to travel over rocky, uneven surfaces. Winter tires have treads that provide traction in icy conditions. Most racing tires have no treads at all. They are

Deeper treads provide more traction on wet or snowy roads.

completely smooth. This allows them to grip the flat surfaces of a racetrack. This does not work if the track is wet, however. F1 cars use treaded tires when a track is wet and smooth ones when a track is dry. NASCAR races are postponed if the track is wet.

UNDER PRESSURE

The amount of air in a car's tires can have a big impact on handling. Tires with high air pressure are very hard, while tires with low pressure are softer. If the pressure is too high, a car might have trouble gripping the track, making it slide around too much. If it is too low, it might make the car's handling less responsive. Drivers work with their crews to find the perfect balance. A driver who notices that the tires' air pressure is less than perfect during a race might contact the crew chief over the radio so adjustments can be made during the next pit stop. ✺

A NASCAR crew member checks tire pressure during a race.

UNDER THE HOOD

Of course, a car wouldn't get very far without an engine to power it. A professional race team usually builds its engines almost entirely from scratch. Engineers design individual components, and fabricators create them from blank chunks of metal. Engines are built separately from the car itself. They are placed in cars as one of the last steps in the building process.

Professional racing organizations such as NASCAR and Formula One have strict rules about the types of engines that race teams are allowed to put in their cars. This keeps races fair for all teams. However, engines are not exactly the same. Engineers and mechanics think creatively to give their engines the edge over competitors.

F1 mechanics make adjustments to an engine's various parts.

NASCAR CARS ARE LOADED INTO THE UPPER SECTION OF A TRAILER.

NASCAR crews generally travel straight from one race to the next, fine-tuning their cars along the way.

RACE DAY

Once a car is ready to go, it is loaded onto a truck and hauled to the racetrack. For major races, the car might need to arrive a day or more before the race. This time allows race officials to inspect the car and make sure it does not break any rules.

At the track, the team performs final tests on the engine to see that it is working in peak condition. Before a race begins, the driver practices on the track to warm up and test the car. For some races, there might be entire days set aside for practice sessions. After this, the team can perform any necessary last-minute tweaks, such as adjusting the car's suspension or the air pressure in its tires. Team members make sure the engine has fresh spark plugs and plenty of oil. They also make sure the car's **fuel cells** are full.

Finally, the car is ready to go. The team members watch as their driver takes off from the starting line with the engine roaring. Their hard work has paid off, and now it is time to watch the race!

THE FUTURE

The FIA's all-electric championship is called Formula E.

THE FUTURE

Cars have come a long way since they were first invented. The slow, clunky carriages of the late 19th century look like entirely different machines next to today's sleek and speedy racers. As time goes on, automobile manufacturers will continue pushing technology forward in new and exciting ways. Decades from now, race fans might look back on today's cars as being slow and outdated compared to the blazing-fast vehicles of the future.

IT'S ELECTRIC!

In September 2014, the FIA began a brand-new racing championship exclusively for electricity-powered race cars. Instead of burning gasoline, they are powered by rechargeable batteries. Traditional gas-powered engines release chemicals into the air that are harmful to the planet. The FIA hopes that electric cars will catch on as a more environmentally safe form of racing.

The new cars can travel at speeds of up to 137 miles per hour (220 kph). However, future models could be faster. It is even possible that one day, all cars might be powered by electricity.

VISIONS OF TOMORROW

Car designers are always thinking ahead. Even as they are perfecting today's latest technology, they are thinking about things that might only be possible many years from now. They often discuss and show off some of these ideas at auto shows, where car enthusiasts and people involved in the automotive industry gather to check out the latest vehicles.

Sometimes manufacturers create vehicles called concept cars. These cars showcase some of the designers' wildest ideas. They often are not capable of actually being driven. Instead, they offer audiences a glimpse into what the future might hold. For example, in 2008, the car manufacturer BMW showed off a concept car with a body made out of stretchy fabric instead of metal. The fabric was stretched over a metal frame made of many moving parts. This meant the car could actually change shape! While you won't be seeing this car on the road or track anytime soon, it is just one of the countless possibilities for the future of car design. ☀

The fabric that covers BMW's GINA Light Visionary Model resists water and extreme temperatures.

CAREER STATS

AUTOMOTIVE SERVICE TECHNICIANS AND MECHANICS

MEDIAN ANNUAL SALARY (2012): $36,610

NUMBER OF JOBS (2012): 701,100

PROJECTED JOB GROWTH: 9%, as fast as average

PROJECTED INCREASE IN JOBS 2012–2022: 60,400

REQUIRED EDUCATION: High school diploma

LICENSE/CERTIFICATION: Industry certification is usually required

MECHANICAL ENGINEERS

MEDIAN ANNUAL SALARY (2012): $80,580

NUMBER OF JOBS (2012): 258,100

PROJECTED JOB GROWTH: 5%, slower than average

PROJECTED INCREASE IN JOBS 2012–2022: 11,600

REQUIRED EDUCATION: Bachelor's degree

LICENSE/CERTIFICATION: State license, available after four years of experience; test requirements vary by state

INDUSTRIAL DESIGNERS

MEDIAN ANNUAL SALARY (2012): $59,610

NUMBER OF JOBS (2012): 39,200

PROJECTED JOB GROWTH: 4%, slower than average

PROJECTED INCREASE IN JOBS 2012–2022: 1,700

REQUIRED EDUCATION: Bachelor's degree

LICENSE/CERTIFICATION: None

Figures reported by the United States Bureau of Labor Statistics

RESOURCES

BOOKS

Christopher, Matt. *Great Moments in American Auto Racing.* New York: Little, Brown and Co., 2011.

Hantula, Richard. *Science at Work in Auto Racing.* New York: Marshall Cavendish Benchmark, 2012.

Howell, Brian. *Rally Car Racing: Tearing It Up.* Minneapolis: Lerner Publications Company, 2014.

Roberts, Angela. *NASCAR's Greatest Drivers.* New York: Random House, 2009.

FACTS FOR NOW

Visit this Scholastic Web site
for more information on race cars:
www.factsfornow.scholastic.com
Enter the keywords **Race Cars**

GLOSSARY

acceleration (ak-sel-ur-AY-shuhn) the act of moving faster and faster

aerodynamic (air-oh-dye-NAM-ik) designed to move through the air very easily and quickly

chassis (CHAS-ee) the frame of a vehicle, on which the body is assembled

circuit (SUR-kit) a route or trip that ends in the place where it began

cockpit (KAHK-pit) the area where the driver of certain race cars sits

engineers (en-juh-NEERZ) people who are specially trained to design and build machines or large structures such as bridges and roads

fenders (FEN-durz) covers over the wheel of a car or bicycle that protect the wheel against damage and reduce splashing

fuel cells (FYOOL SEHLZ) devices that produce electricity directly from a chemical reaction

handling (HAND-ling) the ease with which a vehicle is controlled

internal combustion engine (in-TUR-nuhl kuhm-BUHS-chuhn IN-juhn) a type of engine that creates energy by burning fuel inside the engine itself

maneuverable (muh-NOO-vuh-ruh-buhl) able to be maneuvered, or moved carefully

mass production (MAS pruh-DUHK-shuhn) the method of making large amounts of identical things with machines in a factory

open-wheeled (OH-puhn WEELD) describing a type of race car in which the wheels stick out to the side of the car's body

prototypes (PROH-tuh-tipes) the first versions of inventions that test an idea to see if it will work

rotors (ROH-turz) the parts of an engine or other machine that turn or rotate

series (SEER-eez) a group of related things, such as individual races, that come one after another

straightaways (STRAYT-uh-wayz) sections of a road or racetrack that don't curve

suspension (suh-SPEN-shuhn) the system in a car that provides stability and improves handling

templates (TEM-plits) shapes or patterns that a person draws or cuts around to make the same shape in another material, such as paper or metal

traction (TRAK-shuhn) the force that keeps a moving body from slipping on a surface

treads (TREDZ) the ridges on a car tire or the sole of a shoe that help prevent slipping

trigonometry (trig-uh-NAH-muh-tree) the mathematical study of triangles

welded (WELD-id) connected two pieces of metal or plastic by heating them until they are soft enough to be joined together

INDEX

Page numbers in *italics* indicate illustrations.

INDEX *(CONTINUED)*

ABOUT THE AUTHOR

JOSH GREGORY writes and edits books for kids. He lives in Chicago, Illinois.